Anonymous

Evening Prayers for the House of Mourning

With thoughts on death and immortality

Anonymous

Evening Prayers for the House of Mourning
With thoughts on death and immortality

ISBN/EAN: 9783337303914

Printed in Europe, USA, Canada, Australia, Japan

Cover: Foto ©Thomas Meinert / pixelio.de

More available books at **www.hansebooks.com**

FOR THE

House of Mourning;

WITH

Thoughts on Death and Immortality.

נחמו נחמו עמי יאמר אלהיכם.

"Comfort ye, comfort ye, my people," saith *your God.*

NEW YORK:

PHILIP COWEN, 498-500 THIRD AVENUE.

1890.

Contents.

A Meditation.

*" We often do more good by our
sympathy than by our labor."*

GOD is nigh to all that call upon Him in
truth ; He hearkeneth to the voice of the
humble and lendeth His ear to the call of the
upright in heart. He answereth those that
wait for Him, and sendeth light and rest to
the longing heart. Every reverent thought
is a blessing ; every act of homage prompted
by our sense of His greatness is a benediction;
no true soul-prayer remains unrewarded.

But the purest offering is that prayer which
springs from our sympathy with the afflicted,
and our compassion with the sorrowing and
bereaved.. For it is free from all selfish
motives ; it is inspired by the love of our
fellowmen and sanctified by our pity with
the suffering. Surely when we are deeply
moved with these feelings, then will the words
of our lips and the meditations of our hearts
be acceptable on high.

Whilst we are assembled with our friends
in 'the shadow that has fallen on their home,
and are entering sincerely into their grief, we

will raise our voices together in prayer to the Father above, beseeching for them His comfort and His strength. They need light in the gloom that has gathered around their hearth ; and whence can it come to them but from the Father of Light ? They need fortitude, patience and resignation under the chastenings of the Lord. Whence can they receive these gifts save from Him who has laid the burden of suffering on them ?

Who amongst us has not passed through similar trials and endured like visitations ? Some bear fresh wounds in their own hearts, and, therefore, feel more keenly the human kinship of sorrow. Others, whose days of trial are more remote, but who have not yet forgotten them, recall the soothing comfort that fellow-feeling brought to their broken spirits. And those who have not yet tasted of the bitter cup cannot know how soon they may be called upon to drink of it. We are travellers on the same road which leads to the same goal. All that we prize most highly is but lent to us for a time, and we must surrender it when the Power above demands. Happy the man that lays this to heart and confides in the power of God alone.

May we not leave unheeded the lessons which every house of mourning teaches:

> Number well thy earthly days,
> Let thy heart to wisdom turn;
> Riches go not with us hence.
> Worldly honors stay behind;
> Practice virtue, walk upright,
> Blissful shall thy end then be.
> For God regards His servant's soul,
> Forsaketh not, who trusts in Him !

" In the day of prosperity be joyful ; but in the day of adversity—consider : God has set the one day over against the other ; He has made this as well as that, and no man can find out what follows after it "—*Ecclesiastes, vii.* 14.

"What? Shall we receive the good at God's hand, and shall we not receive evil? In all this Job did not sin with his lips "—*Job, ii* 10.

Selections

for

Alternate Reading.

THE FIRST EVENING.

Minister.—Praise the Lord, O my soul, and all that is within me, praise His holy name.

Congregation.—Praise the Lord, O my soul, and forget not all His benefits.

M.—He has forgiven thy sins; He has healed thine infirmities; He has saved thy life from destruction and granted thee grace and mercy.

C.—He has not dealt with us after our sins, nor requited us according to our transgressions.

M.—Like a father pitieth his children, so the Lord pitieth those that fear Him.

C.—For He knoweth our frailty; He remembereth that we are dust.

M.—The days of men are as grass; as flowers of the field, so they bloom.

C.—A wind passeth over them and they are gone, and their places know them no more.

M.--But the mercy of God is everlasting and is with those that fear Him.

C.—His righteousness is with the faithful, with those who remember His commandments to do them.

M.—The Lord is enthroned on high, yet hath regard for those who are of an humble and contrite spirit.

C.—He doth not afflict willingly, nor wantonly grieve the children of men.

M.—Hear, O God, those whocall on Thee in their distress ; have mercy upon them and lift up their souls.

C. -Give ear to our words, consider our meditations ; for unto Thee, O God, do we pray.

M.—The Lord is my portion, saith my soul, therefore will I hope in Him. It is good for man to wait patiently for the salvation of God. Let us search our hearts and prove our ways, and let us turn to Him, whose compassion faileth never.

SECOND EVENING.

Minister.—Blessed is the man that trusteth in God ; for He will be his refuge.

Congregation.—Trust in the Lord and do good ; verily thou shalt be satisfied.

M.—Trust in Him at all times, ye yeople, pour out your hearts before Him.

C.—Commit thy ways unto the Lord and He will order all things well.

M.—Show me Thy way, O Lord, teach me Thy paths and lead me in Thy truth.

C.—The counsel of the Lord is with those that fear Him and He will show them His faithfulness.

M.—When the troubles of my heart are increased, O bring me out of my distress.

C.—Wait on the Lord, be of good courage and He shall strengthen Thy heart.

M.—Create in me a pure heart and renew a right spirit within me.

C.—Restore unto me the joy of Thy salvation and uphold me with Thy beneficent spirit.

M.—When many thoughts perplex me, Thy comforts delight my soul.

C.—They that know Thy name will put their trust in Thee, for Thou, O Lord, wilt not forsake those that seek Thee

M.—He granteth power to the faint, and to those that have no might He giveth new strength.

C.—My times are in Thy hand and Thou wilt guide and sustain me even unto the end.

Minister:

FOR the mountains may depart and the hills be removed, saith the Lord, but My kindness shall not depart nor My covenant of peace be removed from thee. Who is among you that feareth the Lord, that walketh in darkness and has no light? Let him trust in God, and his heart rest upon Him. Despise not the chastening of the Lord, neither be thou weary of His corrections; for the Lord still loveth those whom he chastiseth, even as a father his son in whom his soul delighteth.

Goodness and mercy follow me all the days of my life and I shall dwell in the Eternal House of God forever.

THIRD EVENING.

Minister.—I will extol the Lord at all times, His praise shall be continually in my mouth.

Congregation.—How excellent is His name in all the earth! He has set His glory above the heavens.

M.—When I consider Thy heavens, sun, moon and stars which Thou hast made.

C.—O what is man, that Thou rememberest him and the son of man that Thou shouldst regard him!

M.—Behold his days are as the span of the hand, his age is as nothing before Thee.

C.—Verily, every man at his best estate is altogether vanity.

M.—Lord, make me know my end, and the measure of my days, what it is, that I may remember how frail I am.

C.—I have set the Lord constantly before me; He is at my right hand, I shall not be moved.

M.—Into Thy hand I commit my spirit; do unto me as seemeth best in Thy sight.

C.—He healeth the broken hearted and bindeth up their wounds.

M.—Mine eyes are unto Thee, O God, leave not my soul destitute.

C.—I will wait patiently for the Lord; for He will incline His ear unto my cry.

M.—He is my light and my strength; He will lead me and bring me out of my darkness.

C.—Fear thou not, for I am with thee; be not dismayed, for I will strengthen and uphold thee.

Minister :

The Everlasting God, the Creator of the ends of the earth, fainteth not, neither is He weary. Seek ye God while He may be found, call upon Him while He is near; let the sinner forsake his way and the unrighteous man his thoughts, and let him return to the Eternal, and He will have mercy, and unto our God, who will abundantly pardon.

For I know the thoughts which I think concerning you, saith the Lord; they are thoughts of peace, and not of evil, to give you a future and a hope.

בָּרְכוּ אֶת יְיָ הַמְבֹרָךְ :

בָּרוּךְ יְיָ הַמְבֹרָךְ לְעוֹלָם וָעֶד :

בָּרוּךְ אַתָּה יְיָ אֱלֹהֵינוּ מֶלֶךְ הָעוֹלָם אֲשֶׁר בִּדְבָרוֹ
מַעֲרִיב עֲרָבִים בְּחָכְמָה פוֹתֵחַ שְׁעָרִים וּבִתְבוּנָה
מְשַׁנֶּה עִתִּים וּמַחֲלִיף אֶת הַזְמַנִּים וּמְסַדֵּר אֶת
הַכּוֹכָבִים בְּמִשְׁמְרֹתֵיהֶם בָּרָקִיעַ כִּרְצוֹנוֹ בּוֹרֵא יוֹם
וָלַיְלָה גּוֹלֵל אוֹר מִפְּנֵי חֹשֶׁךְ וְחֹשֶׁךְ מִפְּנֵי אוֹר
וּמַעֲבִיר יוֹם וּמֵבִיא לַיְלָה וּמַבְדִּיל בֵּין יוֹם וּבֵין לַיְלָה
יְיָ צְבָאוֹת שְׁמוֹ : אֵל חַי וְקַיָּם תָּמִיד יִמְלוֹךְ עָלֵינוּ
לְעוֹלָם וָעֶד : בָּרוּךְ אַתָּה יְיָ הַמַּעֲרִיב עֲרָבִים :

אַהֲבַת עוֹלָם בֵּית יִשְׂרָאֵל עַמְּךָ אָהָבְתָּ תּוֹרָה
וּמִצְוֹת חֻקִּים וּמִשְׁפָּטִים אוֹתָנוּ לִמַּדְתָּ עַל כֵּן יְיָ
אֱלֹהֵינוּ בְּשָׁכְבֵּנוּ וּבְקוּמֵנוּ נָשִׂיחַ בְּחֻקֶּיךָ וְנִשְׂמַח
בְּדִבְרֵי תוֹרָתֶךָ וּבְמִצְוֹתֶיךָ לְעוֹלָם וָעֶד כִּי הֵם חַיֵּינוּ
וְאֹרֶךְ יָמֵינוּ וּבָהֶם נֶהְגֶּה יוֹמָם וָלַיְלָה וְאַהֲבָתְךָ אַל
תָּסִיר מִמֶּנּוּ לְעוֹלָמִים : בָּרוּךְ אַתָּה יְיָ אוֹהֵב עַמּוֹ
יִשְׂרָאֵל :

Evening Services.

Let us worship God and praise His name.

Praised be the Lord, now and forever.

O Eternal. our God, Ruler of all nature, with wisdom Thou openest the gates of the morning, makest the day to fade into the evening and the evening to grow into the night ; and causest the changes of time and the alternations of seasons. The stars hast Thou placed in the firmament and ordained their courses; by the greatness of Thy power not one faileth. Thine is the day and Thine the night; darkness and light are alike before Thee. We thank Thee for the day and its work, for the night and its rest.

Infinite as is Thy power, even so is Thy love. Thou madest it manifest to mankind through Thy servant Israel, whom Thou didst guide to the knowledge of Thy being and unto whom Thou didst reveal Thy law of holiness. Therefore, at our lying down and our rising up, we will meditate on Thy commandments, and with gladness think upon the teachings of Thy word. Therein we shall

שְׁמַע יִשְׂרָאֵל יְהוָֹה אֱלֹהֵינוּ יְהוָֹה אֶחָד׃

וְאָהַבְתָּ אֵת יְיָ אֱלֹהֶיךָ בְּכָל לְבָבְךָ וּבְכָל נַפְשְׁךָ וּבְכָל מְאֹדֶךָ׃ וְהָיוּ הַדְּבָרִים הָאֵלֶּה אֲשֶׁר אָנֹכִי מְצַוְּךָ הַיּוֹם עַל לְבָבֶךָ׃ וְשִׁנַּנְתָּם לְבָנֶיךָ וְדִבַּרְתָּ בָּם בְּשִׁבְתְּךָ בְּבֵיתֶךָ וּבְלֶכְתְּךָ בַדֶּרֶךְ וּבְשָׁכְבְּךָ וּבְקוּמֶךָ׃ וּקְשַׁרְתָּם לְאוֹת עַל יָדֶךָ וְהָיוּ לְטֹטָפֹת בֵּין עֵינֶיךָ וּכְתַבְתָּם עַל מְזֻזוֹת בֵּיתֶךָ וּבִשְׁעָרֶיךָ׃

אֱמֶת וֶאֱמוּנָה כָּל זֹאת וְקַיָּם עָלֵינוּ כִּי הוּא יְיָ אֱלֹהֵינוּ וְאֵין זוּלָתוֹ וַאֲנַחְנוּ יִשְׂרָאֵל עַמּוֹ׃ הַפּוֹדֵנוּ מִיַּד מְלָכִים מַלְכֵּנוּ הַגּוֹאֲלֵנוּ מִכַּף כָּל הֶעָרִיצִים׳ הָעֹשֶׂה גְדוֹלוֹת עַד אֵין חֵקֶר וְנִפְלָאוֹת עַד אֵין מִסְפָּר׳ הַשָּׂם נַפְשֵׁנוּ בַּחַיִּים וְלֹא נָתַן לַמּוֹט רַגְלֵנוּ׳ הָעֹשֶׂה לָנוּ נִסִּים בְּמִצְרַיִם אוֹתוֹת וּמוֹפְתִים בְּאַדְמַת בְּנֵי חָם׳ וַיַּרְאוּ בָנָיו גְּבוּרָתוֹ שִׁבְּחוּ וְהוֹדוּ לִשְׁמוֹ׳

find true life, strength according to our needs
and comfort in the day of trouble. Blessed be
Thou, O God, for the revelation of Thy love
unto Israel.

Congregation:

Hear. O Israel, the Eternal our God, the
Eternal is One.

Minister:

Thou shalt love the Eternal, thy God, with
all thy heart, and with all thy soul, and with
all thy might. And those words which I,
the Lord, have commanded thee shall forever
dwell in thy heart. Thou shalt be diligent in
teaching them to thy children. Thou shalt
speak of them when thou sittest in thy house,
when thou walkest by the way, when thou
liest down and when thou risest up. Let
them be as a sign upon thy hand, as a guide
before thine eyes and as a memorial upon
the doorposts of thy house and the gates of
thy city.

True is this, and we believe it as did our
fathers. The Eternal is our God, and there
is none besides Him. He hath redeemed Israel
from the power of kings and hath delivered
him from the hands of oppressors. He hath
done for us great things without measure and
wonderful things without number. He has

מִי כָמֹכָה בָּאֵלִים יְיָ מִי כָּמֹכָה נֶאְדָּר בַּקֹּדֶשׁ נוֹרָא תְהִלֹת עֹשֵׂה פֶלֶא׳

מַלְכוּתְךָ רָאוּ בָנֶיךָ׳ בּוֹקֵעַ יָם לִפְנֵי מֹשֶׁה׃ זֶה אֵלִי עָנוּ וְאָמְרוּ׃

יְיָ יִמְלֹךְ לְעֹלָם וָעֶד׃

וְנֶאֱמַר כִּי פָדָה יְיָ אֶת יַעֲקֹב וּגְאָלוֹ מִיַּד חָזָק מִמֶּנּוּ׃ בָּרוּךְ אַתָּה יְיָ גָּאַל יִשְׂרָאֵל׃

בָּרוּךְ אַתָּה יְיָ אֱלֹהֵינוּ וֵאלֹהֵי אֲבוֹתֵינוּ אֱלֹהֵי אַבְרָהָם אֱלֹהֵי יִצְחָק וֵאלֹהֵי יַעֲקֹב הָאֵל הַגָּדוֹל הַגִּבּוֹר וְהַנּוֹרָא אֵל עֶלְיוֹן קֹנֵה שָׁמַיִם וָאָרֶץ׃ מְכַלְכֵּל חַיִּים בְּחֶסֶד סוֹמֵךְ נוֹפְלִים וְרוֹפֵא חוֹלִים וּמַתִּיר אֲסוּרִים וּמְקַיֵּם אֱמוּנָתוֹ לִישֵׁנֵי עָפָר׃

wrought signs and wonders in Egypt, parting also the sea before Moses and the children of Israel. And seeing the signs of His power they gave praise to Him and exclaimed: "This is my God, I will extol Him; the God of my fathers, and I will exalt Him.

Congregation:

Who is like unto Thee, O God, among the mighty? Who can be compared unto Thee in holiness, in awe-inspiring power, in deeds of wonder?

Minister:

As Thou hast redeemed Israel and saved him from arms stronger than his, so mayest Thou send redemption to all people who are oppressed and persecuted, and grant them the blessings of liberty, of justice and of peace.

OUR God, and God of our fathers, the Most High, in whose keeping are the heavens and the earth: in mercy Thou sustainest the living, upholdest the falling, pardonest the sinner, healest the sick, liftest up those who are bowed down; Thou wilt surely fulfil the promise of immortality which Thou hast implanted in our being.

אַתָּה חוֹנֵן לְאָדָם דַּעַת וּמְלַמֵּד לֶאֱנוֹשׁ בִּינָה אָנָּא יְיָ
הֲבִינֵנוּ דְרָכֶיךָ וּמוֹל אֶת לְבָבֵנוּ לְיִרְאָה אֶת שְׁמָךְ ׳
סְלַח וּמְחַל לָנוּ וְהָסֵר מִמֶּנּוּ יָגוֹן וַאֲנָחָה ׳ בָּרֵךְ שְׁנָתֵנוּ
וְאַרְצֵנוּ ׳ נִדָּחִים תְּקַבֵּץ ׳ וְהַתּוֹעִים עַל דַּעְתְּךָ יִשָׁפֵטוּ
וְיִשְׂמְחוּ צַדִּיקִים כִּישׁוּעָתֶךָ ׳ טֶרֶם נִקְרָא אַתָּה תַעֲנֶה ׳
כִּי אַתָּה יְיָ עוֹנֶה בְּכָל עֵת ׳ פּוֹדֶה וּמַצִּיל מִכָּל צָרָה
וְצוּקָה :

———

בָּרוּךְ יְהֹוָה בַּיּוֹם ׳ בָּרוּךְ יְהֹוָה בַּלַּיְלָה ׳ בָּרוּךְ יְהֹוָה
בְּשָׁכְבֵנוּ ׳ בָּרוּךְ יְהֹוָה בְּקוּמֵנוּ ׳ כִּי בְיָדְךָ נַפְשׁוֹת
הַחַיִּים וְהַמֵּתִים ׳ בְּיָדְךָ נֶפֶשׁ כָּל חַי וְרוּחַ כָּל בְּשַׂר
אִישׁ ׳ בְּשָׁלוֹם יַחְדָּו אֶשְׁכְּבָה וְאִישָׁן ׳ כִּי אַתָּה
יְהֹוָה לְבָדָד לָבֶטַח תּוֹשִׁיבֵנִי ׳ יְהֹוָה לִי וְלֹא אִירָא :
אֲנִי בְּצֶדֶק אֶחֱזֶה פָנֶיךָ ׳ אֶשְׂבְּעָה בְהָקִיץ תְּמוּנָתֶךָ ׳

THOU, O gracious God, bestowest knowledge on man and endowest him with understanding. Be pleased to send us Thy light and Thy truth that we gain an ever clearer insight into the wisdom of Thy ways. Help us to banish every desire and thought of evil, and truly to reverence Thy holy name. Forgive us our trespasses, pardon our sins ; and may the pain of remorse for our misdoings make us more watchful and more firm in resisting temptations   May the erring and the wayward be led to know, to fear and to serve Thee, and those who love virtue and do the right ever be glad in Thy favor. Bless this our land with plenty and our nation with peace, and may the spirit of brotherhood reign amongst us.   O, Thou, who knowest our needs before we utter them, and ordainest all things for the best, to Thee we look as our deliverer in all times of trouble and distress.

הַשְׁכִּיבֵנוּ יְיָ אֱלֹהֵינוּ לְשָׁלוֹם וְהַעֲמִידֵנוּ מַלְכֵּנוּ
לְחַיִּים וּפְרוֹשׂ עָלֵינוּ סֻכַּת שְׁלוֹמֶךָ וְהַקְּנֵנוּ בְּעֵצָה
טוֹבָה מִלְּפָנֶיךָ וְהוֹשִׁיעֵנוּ לְמַעַן שְׁמֶךָ וְהָגֵן בַּעֲדֵנוּ
וְהָסֵר מֵעָלֵינוּ אוֹיֵב דֶּבֶר וְחֶרֶב וְרָעָב וְיָגוֹן וּבְצֵל
כְּנָפֶיךָ תַּסְתִּירֵנוּ כִּי אֵל שׁוֹמְרֵנוּ וּמַצִּילֵנוּ אָתָּה כִּי
אֵל מֶלֶךְ חַנּוּן וְרַחוּם אָתָּה וּשְׁמוֹר צֵאתֵנוּ וּבוֹאֵנוּ
לְחַיִּים וּלְשָׁלוֹם מֵעַתָּה וְעַד עוֹלָם ׳

עֲנֵנוּ יְיָ עֲנֵנוּ ׳ וְאַל תִּתְעַלַּם מִתְּחִנָּתֵנוּ ׳ הֱיֵה נָא
קָרוֹב לְקוֹרְאֶיךָ ׳ שְׁלַח מַרְפֵּא לְתַחֲלוּאֵי יָדֶיךָ ׳ יְהִי
נָא חַסְדְּךָ לְנַחֵם הָאֻמְלָלִים וְלַחֲבשׁ שֶׁבֶר לִבָּם ׳ כִּי
אַתָּה יְיָ תִּמְחֹץ וְיָדֶיךָ תִּרְפֶּאנָה ׳ בָּרוּךְ אַתָּה יְיָ מְנַחֵם
אֲבֵלִים :

For the Night.

GRANT, O heavenly Father, that we lie down for our nightly rest with a quiet mind, and rise again in the morning in health and strength, to take up the duties of the new day. May Thy protection be a shield around our homes during our sleeping hours. Preserve. us from evil occurrences, from the sword of the foe, from civil troubles, from pestilence, famine and destruction. May we put aside all our cares and surrender our lives and the lives of our loved ones into Thy keeping. May we readily forgive those who wronged us, and seek forgiveness of those whom we have wronged. So shall thy blessing attend the closing and the opening days, and Thy peace, O God, abide within us.

———

Hear, O God, and answer us; turn not thine ear from our supplications; be near to us when we call on Thee, mercifully to comfort the afflicted and bind up the wounds of their hearts.

Congregation: •

Amen.

The Adoration.

ALMIGHTY GOD, Thou hast created the world in wisdom: Thou guidest the destinies of man with a just and wise purpose. As a father dost Thou love us and bestow on us unceasing mercies. Even when thou sendest us trials, yea, makest us suffer bereavement, we will not doubt that Thy doings are right and that Thy chastenings are meant for good and not for evil. In our griefs as in our joys we acknowledge Thy power, that giveth and taketh away.

Congregation :

Before Thee we bow the head and bend the knee, and humbly resign ourselves to Thy holy decrees.

Minister:

We remember that we are only pilgrims upon this earth; that it is our duty to walk in

Thy ways, to do what is good in Thy sight, to keep our souls pure from sin ; and when Thou callest us hence, attain that reward which is prepared for those who have earnestly striven to live in accordance with Thy will. To Thee we look for comfort and strength when one of our beloved is taken from us, and a link broken in the chain of love that binds us together in family union. And when our time comes to walk into the valley of the shadow of death, we will fear no evil, for Thou art with us in death as in life, here and hereafter.

Blessed be Thou, O Eternal, our God, in all Thy dispensations; and hallowed shall be Thy name, whatsoever Thou mayest send us.

(Here the Minister may add a special prayer befitting the occasion

יִתְגַּדַּל וְיִתְקַדַּשׁ שְׁמֵהּ רַבָּא בְּעָלְמָא דִּי־בְרָא
כִרְעוּתֵהּ וְיַמְלִיךְ מַלְכוּתֵהּ בְּחַיֵּיכוֹן וּבְיוֹמֵיכוֹן וּבְחַיֵּי
דְכָל בֵּית יִשְׂרָאֵל בַּעֲגָלָא וּבִזְמַן קָרִיב וְאִמְרוּ אָמֵן:

יְהֵא שְׁמֵהּ רַבָּא מְבָרַךְ לְעָלַם וּלְעָלְמֵי עָלְמַיָּא יִתְבָּרַךְ
וְיִשְׁתַּבַּח וְיִתְפָּאַר וְיִתְרוֹמַם וְיִתְנַשֵּׂא וְיִתְהַדָּר וְיִתְעַלֶּה
וְיִתְהַלָּל שְׁמֵהּ דְקוּדְשָׁא בְּרִיךְ הוּא לְעֵלָּא וּלְעֵלָּא מִן
כָּל בִּרְכָתָא וְשִׁירָתָא תֻּשְׁבְּחָתָא וְנֶחֱמָתָא דַּאֲמִירָן
בְּעָלְמָא וְאִמְרוּ אָמֵן·

עַל יִשְׂרָאֵל וְעַל צַדִּיקַיָּא וְעַל כָּל מַן דְּאִתְפְּטַר
מִן עָלְמָא הָדֵין כִּרְעוּתֵיהּ דֶּאֱלָהָא· יְהֵא לְהוֹן
שְׁלָמָא רַבָּא וְחוּלָקָא טָבָא לְחַיֵּי עָלְמָא דְּאָרְתֵּי·
וְחִסְדָּא וְרַחֲמֵי מִן קָדָם מָרֵא שְׁמַיָּא וְאַרְעָא·
וְאִמְרוּ אָמֵן:
יְהֵא שְׁלָמָא רַבָּא מִן שְׁמַיָּא וְחַיִּים עָלֵינוּ וְעַל כָּל
יִשְׂרָאֵל וְאִמְרוּ אָמֵן:
עֹשֶׂה שָׁלוֹם בִּמְרוֹמָיו הוּא יַעֲשֶׂה שָׁלוֹם עָלֵינוּ
וְעַל כָּל יִשְׂרָאֵל וְאִמְרוּ אָמֵן:

(The mourners join the Minister.)

The Kaddeesh.

EXTOLLED and hallowed be the name of the Almighty throughout the world which He has created according to His righteous will. May His kingdom come nearer with its redeeming power and spread over the earth through the testimony of Israel, His servant.

Congregation :
AMEN. May His holy name be praised in all the world and for evermore.

Minister :
To the departed   may there be peace in the realms of eternal life; may resting from   labors, partake of the bliss in the other world. There may   find grace and mercy, and may   memory be for blessing with those whose love reaches beyond the tomb. Our good deeds live after us ; our righteous walk worketh righteousness, and our love is not lost in the grave.

May He, who is the giver of peace, grant peace to all troubled souls, and comfort all the bereaved amongst us.

Congregation :
AMEN.

Thoughts

on

Death and Immortality.

Thoughts on Death and Immortality.

RESIGNATION.

The Rabbi Meier was one of the great teachers in Israel, whose name is celebrated even to this day. His wisdom and piety had gathered round him a large number of scholars, who never failed to be with him as he expounded the law, and taught, from the stores of his well filled mind, the memorable sayings of the sages and rabbis of the olden time. One sabbath he was as usual with his pupils in the synagogue, and was specially interested in the lesson which he was giving; his scholars were so eager to obtain all the information possible and so hung upon every word he spoke, that the hour grew late and later before he left the hall and returned home.

He had a happy home. God had blessed him with a wife who loved him with all the tenderness of which a woman's heart is capable and with two boys growing up in piety and intelligence. When he had left home in the morning for his duties in the synagogue, the boys were well; but who can tell what a day will bring forth? A sudden illness fell upon them, and although the poor mother did all she could to relieve their agony, in one short hour they breathed their last. Grief and death had entered the dwelling, and the poor mother stood petrified by her sorrow. not knowing what to do. Should she meet her husband on his way from the synagogue with the sad tale, or leave him for the few hours that would elapse before the close of the day, to remain in happy ignorance? At last she determined to await his return, and, having again turned to the bodies of her beloved children, she once more tried to discover a sign of life. Alas! the feather lay unmoved upon their lips; no spot dimmed the bright surface of the mirror—they were dead, and she had to wrestle in prayer for strength to bear her sorrow in patience. She was a truly devout woman, and while she could but groan over her loss, she set about her duties; she placed the two lads upon the bed, and covered their faces with a shroud; often she prayed for strength to be able to meet her husband and prepare him for the blow he would have to bear. She closed the door behind her and entered the room adjoining, struggling in spirit to conceal her grief.

At last Rabbi Meier returned; as soon as he entered the room he looked round, 'Where are my sons?'' said he. With a weakened, trembling voice the mother said, "Did you not leave them with the other scholars in the synagogue?'' and as she spoke, she dared not lift her eyes lest her husband should see her tearful look, and read in her face the message of his coming woe. "No," he replied, "I did not; I was surprised not to see them in their usual place, and wondered what had kept them away."

His wife said "No?'' but handed to him the wine and the taper for the Habdala*, that he might invoke the blessing of the Eternal for the coming week

Unaccustomed to miss his children, the Rabbi had no sooner concluded the prayer, than he began again to inquire after them; but his wife, knowing that he must be ex-

---

* The Habdala is a religious ceremony, which is performed on the evening of the Sabbath, at the hour when the holy day is drawing to a close, and the time is beginning when labor is again permitted. It is a prayer invoking the blessing of God upon the coming week; and a lighted taper, wine, and frankincense are used in it as emblems of the rich bene · fits which God gives as the reward of labor.

hausted by the fatigues of the day, again
evaded the question, and urged him to sit
down to his evening meal. He asked a blessing upon the provision set before him; but
having soon satisfied himself and returned
thanks, he asked again for the boys, express-
ing his surprise at their unusual absence, and
asking his wife for an explanation, if she
could give it. Instead of meeting this inquiry,
she said she had to ask his advice about a
subject which caused her much uneasiness of
mind, and which she believed he would be
able to counsel her upon, from his deep
studies of the law. He was all attention, and
then she told him how a dear friend had
sometime ago visited her, and had given into
her charge some very beautiful and precious
jewels. He had not said when he should ask
for them again, and she had almost forgotten
that they were lent to her, so much had she
accustomed herself to enjoy their beauty.
This evening he had called in suddenly, and
asked for the treasure he had left in her
charge. She wished to know whether, as no
time had been fixed to give them back, she
was really obliged to restore them. Rabbi
Meier was startled. "Why," said he, "the

very question is sinful." "But," said she, "I am so fond of these jewels " "They are not yours, however fond you may be of them." "But," said she, "they are so very dear to me, perhaps to you also." "Wife," said the Rabbi, beginning to dread something, he hardly knew what, "What do you mean by these strange doubts? I never heard you utter such sinful thoughts before. Even to *think* of keeping something entrusted to your care is dishonest."

"It is true," said the poor woman, unable to restrain the tears that had been nearly bursting forth before, " But if I must restore the precious jewels, you must help me to bear the loss," and while she spoke she took her wondering husband by the hand, opened the door and led him into the adjoining room, and standing by the bedside, she lifted up the pall, exclaiming amid her sobs, "Behold the jewels; God has demanded them again."

"My children! Both my boys! The joy of my life, the light of my eyes, oh my children!" and the poor father burst into tears.

"Did you not tell me, my husband, did you not tell me that when the owner asks for his own again we must restore it," said the wife, the tears streaming from her eyes, which still, with ineffable tenderness, looked upon her husband.

The bereaved father struggled with the bitterness of his grief, but touched by her thoughtful wisdom exclaimed, "O God, how do I dare to murmur against Thy righteous will ! Thou hast taken from me my children, but hast thou not made me see, even more clearly than before, the piety and the love of my wife!"

And in the chamber of death, the bereaved ones felt that their sorrow had brought them nearer to each other, and closer, too, to God, and they prayed for the strength they so much needed, saying with the patriarch Job,— "The Lord gave, the Lord hath taken away ; blessed be the name of the Lord."—(*From the Talmud, by the Rev. Alfred Steinthal, Manchester, England.*)

———

Rabbi Simeon said : "There are three crowns of honor ; the crown of the knowledge of the Law of God, the crown of priesthood and the crown of royalty ; but the crown of a good name excelleth them all."

Rabbi Jacob said : "This world is the ante-chamber of the world hereafter ; prepare thyself in the ante-chamber that thou mayest enter the hall of the palace.''

Rabbi Eliezer Hakkapor said : " Those born into the world are destined to die ; the dead, to live again, and those who enter the eternal life to be judged. Therefore let it be recognized, understood and remembered, that the Creator is the counsellor, He the judge, He the witness, He the accuser ; He is always ready to give judgment ; blessed be He ! For before Him there is no injustice, no oversight, no regard for rank, no bribery. Know that everything will appear in the account. Accept not the assurance of thy passions that the grave will be a place of refuge for thee. For without thy consent wast thou created, wast born into the world without thy choice ; thou art now living without thy own volition, and without thy approval thou wilt die ; so likewise, without thy consent thou wilt have to render account before the Supreme King, the holy One, blessed be He.''

(*Sayings of the Jewish Fathers.*)

"There are treasures laid up in the heart,— treasures of charity, piety, temperance and soberness. These treasures a man takes with him beyond death, when he leaves this world.''

"The effect of water poured on the root of a tree is seen *aloft in the branches and fruit ;* so in the next world are seen the effects of good deeds performed here.'' *Indian.*

"I consider this world as a place which nature never intended for my permanent abode ; and I look on my departure from it, not as being driven from my habitation, but simply as leaving an inn.'' *Cicero.*

"I trouble not myself about the manner of future existence. I content myself with believing, even to positive conviction, that the Power which gave me existence is able to continue it in any form or manner He pleases, either with or without this body ; and it appears more probable to me that I shall continue to exist hereafter than that I should have existence as I now have, before that existence began. *Theodore Parker.*

"There is a voice from the tomb sweeter than song. There is a remembrance of the dead to which we turn even from the charm of the living. Oh the grave ! It buries every

error, covers every defect. extinguishes every
resentment ! From its peaceful bosom spring
none but fond regrets and tender recollections.

Aye, go to the grave of buried love, and
meditate ! There settle the account with thy
conscience for every past benefit unrequited,
every past endearment unregarded, of that
departed being who can never—never—never
return to be soothed by thy contrition !

Then weave thy chaplet of flowers and
strew the beauties of nature about the grave ;
console thy broken spirit, if thou canst, with
these tender yet futile tributes of regret ; but
take warning by the bitterness of this thy
contrite affliction over the dead and henceforth
be more faithful and affectionate in the dis-
charge of thy duties to the living.

Washington Irving.

"Of what import this vacant sky, these
puffing elements, these insignificant lives,
full of selfish loves and quarrels and ennui ?
Everything is prospective, and man is to live
hereafter. That the world is for his education
is the only sane solution of the enigma. All
the comfort I have found teaches me to con-
fide that I shall not have less in times and

places I do not yet know. I have known
admirable persons, without feeling that they
exhaust the possibilities of virtue and talent.
I have seen glories of climate, of summer
mornings and evenings, of midnight sky ; I
have enjoyed the benefits of all this complex
machinery of arts and civilization and its re-
sults of comfort. The Good Power can easily
provide me millions more as good All I have
seen teaches me to *trust the Creator for all I
have not seen.*"   *Emerson.*

"Fear not the sentence of death ; remember
them that have been before thee and that shall
come after thee ; for this is the law of God
over all flesh.   Have regard to thy name ; for
that shall remain with thee beyond a thousand
treasures of gold."   *Ecclesiasticus.*

On parent knee, a naked newborn child,
Weeping thou satst, while all around thee smiled ;
So live that sinking in thy long last sleep
Thou then mayest smile, while all around thee weep.
                              Oriental.

"Duties are ours ; events are God's.   This
removes an infinite burden from the shoulders

of a miserable, tempted, dying creature. On this consideration only can he securely lay down his head and close his eyes. *Cecil.*

————

TO MYSELF.

Let nothing make thee sad or fretful,
 Or too regretful;
  Be still.

What God hath ordered must be right;
 Then find in it thine own delight,
  My will.

Why shouldst thou fill to day with sorrow
 About to-morrow,
  My heart?

One watches all with care most true;
 Doubt not that He will give thee too
  Thy part.

Only be steadfast : never waver,   .
 Nor seek earth's favor,
  But rest.

Thou knowest what God wills must be
 For all His creatures, so for thee
  The best.

BE STILL MY HEART.

I will commit my way. O Lord to Thee,
Nor doubt Thy love, though dark the way may be,
Nor murmur, for the sorrow is from God,
And there is comfort also in Thy rod.

I will not seek to know the future years,
Nor cloud today with dark tomorrow's fears;
I will but ask a light from heaven, to show
How, step by step, my pilgrimage should go.

And if the distant perils seem to make
The path impossible that I must take,
Yet as the river winds through mountains lone
The way will open up—as I go on.

Be still my heart, for faithful is the Lord,
And pure and true and tried His holy word;
Through stormy flood that rages as the sea,
His promises thy stepping stones shall be.

————

COMFORT.

Whate'er my God ordains is right,
   His will is ever just;
Howe'er He orders now my cause,
   I will be still and trust.
     He is my God;
     Though dark my road,
He holds me that I shall not fall;
Wherefore to him I leave it all.

Whate'er my God ordains is right,
 He never will deceive ;
He leads me by His own right path,
 And so to him I cleave :
 And take, content,
 What He hath sent :
His hands can turn my griefs away,
And patiently I wait His day.

Whate'er my God ordains is right,
 Though I the cup must drink ;
That bitter seems to my faint heart,
 I will not fear nor shrink :
 Tears pass away
 With dawn of day ;
Sweet comfort yet shall fill my heart,
And pain and sorrow all depart.

———

IT SINGETH LOW IN EVERY HEART.

It singeth low in every heart,
 We hear it each and all,—
A song of those who answer not,
 However we may call ;
They throng the silence of the breast,
 We see them as of yore,—
The kind, the brave, the true, the sweet,
 Who walk with us no more.

'Tis hard to take the burden up,
　　When these have laid it down ;
They brightened all the joy of life,
　　They softened every frown ;
But oh, 'tis good to think of them,
　　When we are troubled sore !
Thanks be to God that such have been,
　　Although they are no more !

More homelike seems the vast unknown,
　　Since they have entered there,
To follow them were not so hard,
　　Wherever they may fare ;
. They cannot be where God is not,
　　On any sea or shore ;
Whate'er betides, Thy love abides
　　Our God, for evermore.

J. W. CHADWICK.

HE WHO DIED AT AZIM.

He who died at Azim sends
This to comfort all his friends :
Faithful friends ! It lies, I know,
Pale and white, and cold as snow ;
And ye say, " Abdallah's dead ! "
Weeping at the feet and head,
I can see your falling tears,
I can hear your sighs and prayers ;

Yet I smile and whisper this,—
" I am not the thing you kiss :
Cease your tears and let it lie :
It was mine, it is not I."
Sweet friends ! what the women lave,
For the last sleep of the grave,
Is a hut which I am quitting
Is a garment no more fitting
Is a cage from which at last,
Like a bird my soul hath passed.
Love the inmate, not the room,—
The wearer, not the garb,—the plume
Of the eagle, not the bars,
That kept him from those splendid stars.

Loving friends ! be wise and dry
Straightway every weeping eye.
What ye lift upon the bier
Is not worth a single tear.
'Tis an empty sea shell,—one
Out of which the pearl has gone.
The shell is broken, it lies there :
The pearl, the all, the soul, is here.
'Tis an earthen jar, whose lid
Allah sealed, the while it hid
That treasure of his treasury,
A mind that loved him ; let it lie !
Let the shard be earth's once more,
Since the gold is in his store !

Allah glorious !   Allah good !
Now thy world is understood ;
Now the long, long wonder ends ;
Yet ye weep, my foolish friends,
While the man whom ye call dead,
In unspoken bliss, instead,
Lives and loves you,—lost 'tis true,
For the ligh· that shines for you ;
But in the light ye cannot see
Of undistu·bed felicity,—
In a perfect paradise,
And a life that never dies.
Farewell friends !   But not farewell :
Where I am, ye, too, shall dwell.
I am gone before your face,
A moment's worth, a little space.
When ye come where I have stepped,
Ye will wonder why ye wept :
Ye will know, by true love taught,
That here is all, and there is naught.
Weep awhile, if ye are fain :
Sunshine still must follow rain ;
Only not at death,—for death,
Now we know, is that first breath
Which our souls draw when we enter
Life which is of all life centre.

He who died at Azim gave
This to those who made his grave.

Edwin Arnold